There's a Healer
in the House

There's a Healer in the House

Dr. Ed Dufresne

Ed Dufresne Ministries
Temecula, California

Unless otherwise indicated, all scriptural quotations are from the *King James Version* of the Bible.

Contents

Preface

The House of Healing

By Nancy Dufresne

Recently, I was meditating on the scripture found in Isaiah 53:4 and 5, reading:

> **Surely he hath borne our griefs [sicknesses], and carried our sorrows [diseases]: yet we did esteem him stricken, smitten of God, and afflicted.**

> **But he was wounded for our transgressions, he was bruised for our iniquities: the chastisement of our peace was upon him; and with his stripes we are healed.**

Not only did Jesus die for our *sins* when He was on the cross of Calvary, but He also purchased *healing* for us by the stripes He took on His back.

As salvation is now available through Jesus' sacrifice on Calvary for every human who has lived since then and will ever live on the face of the earth, so healing is also available for every human who will ever live.

The only reason everyone isn't healed is the same reason everyone isn't born again: *They don't know they can be.*

Healing belongs to everyone, but it must be accepted and received, just as salvation belongs to everyone, but it must be accepted and received.

Jesus' House of Healing

At a time in my life when I needed a healing in my body, I was reading the wonderful passage in Isaiah quoted above. When the stripes were laid on Jesus' back, they constituted *payment in full* for any healing I would ever need!

As I continued to meditate on this passage, I asked the Holy Spirit for a greater personal revelation of what belongs to me because of the stripes Jesus took for me.

You never know so much that you can't receive more revelation from the Spirit of God, no matter how familiar a passage seems. Furthermore, you must gain revelation of the Word of God for *yourself.* You can't live off the revelation God gave someone else. The revelation they gain certainly blesses and helps your understanding, but it's only the Holy Spirit who can make it come alive to you.

I told the Holy Spirit, "I know that I was healed two thousand years ago at that moment in time when Jesus took those stripes on His back, but I'm going to meditate on this truth so it will become ingrained in me."

And as I was thinking on that passage of scripture, the Holy Spirit asked me this question: "If someone bought you a house, paid for it in full, and gave you the title deed to it, but you didn't actually move into the house, or take physical possession of it until five years later, when did the house *belong* to you — when the title deed was given to you, or when you moved into it?"

I replied, "When the title deed was given to me."

"Well," continued the Holy Spirit, "Jesus gave you the title deed to your healing two thousand years ago, but you can move into it today."

Did you know that Jesus built you and me a house of healing two thousand years ago? But that house of healing

Jesus built for us will remain vacant until we decide to move into it.

Dealing With Yesterday's "Junk"

Once you buy a house, everything in that house belongs to you. Jesus has provided this marvelous house of healing for us, and everything we will ever need is inside it!

At different times in my life when I moved to a new location, I always noticed as I packed that I had collected so much junk — things that weren't valuable or useful to me but were kept anyway.

I'd start going through my belongings and throwing things away, wondering why I had ever kept them in the first place. Not having to cart useless junk from the old location to the new made the load lighter when I moved.

Second Corinthians 5:17 says, "Therefore if any man be in Christ, he is a new creature: old things are passed away; behold, all things are become new." Hallelujah!

When you were born again, all that "junk" you had collected in your heart was cleaned out. It's not useful to you anymore. You're a brand new creature! You've got no business with the junk of the past! Don't keep any of that old junk belonging to the "old man." As you make life's journey, it will make your load lighter.

When you received Christ as your Savior, He took away that old spirit of death that was on the inside of you and gave you a new spirit, His Spirit of life. Even though all your sins were washed away by His blood, Satan will now try to make you think they aren't gone by bringing them back to your remembrance.

Romans 12:2 says, "...be ye transformed by the renewing of your mind...." That's something *you* must do; God won't do it for you. He gave you a new *spirit*, but you still have your same old *mind* that you must deal with.

The only way to deal with it is by studying the Word of God — building it on the inside of you, knowing it as well as you know your name — and by spending time fellowshipping with God in prayer.

Cleaning Out the Closet of Your Heart

When I threw that junk out at moving time, I took it to the dumpster and left it there.

I could have decided later, "Well, I know that old box of stuff I threw out isn't any good, but it's been around for so long, I'm kind of attached to it. Plus, I never know when I might need it again."

If so, I would have retraced my steps to the dumpster, dug around in the trash, retrieved that worthless box of junk, carted it back into my house, set it down with the other boxes, and said to myself, "Now that's more like it!"

You can do the same thing with that old lifestyle of yours, but you shouldn't.

You receive Jesus as your Savior at the church altar or wherever you are when He comes into your heart (but you certainly don't have to be at an altar to receive Him). Your heart is tender toward Him, and you say, "Jesus, I give you everything. Take my life and make me new again. I don't want to be what I used to be. I give you everything that's displeasing to You and ask You to make me new."

Jesus does just that. Like cleaning out all the old boxes at moving time — in a split second of time, His precious blood floods over your soul.

His Spirit imparts the life of Jesus into your spirit (or heart), and in a moment of time all your unforgiveness, bitterness, hurt, rebellion, and depression is gone. All that extra useless baggage you accumulated throughout your life is discarded.

Jesus goes through the closet of your heart and gets rid of everything you won't need in this new residence of eternal life. You are now that "new creature in Christ" the Bible talks about. Life is sweeter than you ever thought possible!

Avoid the Dumpster of Unforgiveness

However, in just a short amount of time, the devil starts bringing those discarded sins back across your mind. He whispers, "That person you became bitter toward is still just as mean and nasty to you as they ever were. Did you hear what they said to you today? See, nothing has changed. You have a right to feel that way. It's terrible the way they treat you!"

And before you know it, the devil has you marching right back down to the dumpster of unforgiveness and hurt and rummaging through the trash looking for that old, familiar feeling you once possessed.

You cart it back to the living room of your heart that is now the habitation of God's Spirit, and set it down, pushing God's Spirit aside to make room for that old possession of sin.

Resist the Devil

You may ask, "How do I do that? How do I allow that old sin back into my life? I'm a new creature in Christ. He has taken all that old junk away."

Yes, but you can retrieve and bring up that old junk again by talking and thinking about it. And before long, you're reliving those old feelings you had toward that person.

James 4:7 reads, "Submit yourselves therefore to God. Resist the devil, and he will flee from you."

Recognize that those old feelings and thoughts are the nature of the "old man," and the devil wants to pull you back into that "old man" way of thinking and acting again.

Resist him by saying, "No, devil! The new creature that I am won't have fellowship with that old creature. We have nothing in common, and I won't receive those bad thoughts."

Resist the devil!

How To Live in the House of Healing

The house of provision that Jesus built for you to live in not only contains healing as a furnishing; it also contains prosperity, soundness of mind, peace, love, and anything you will need in life.

However, before you move into it, you first must remove any boxes of sin: unforgiveness, bitterness, rebellion, and so forth. You can't bring any sin into Jesus' house. Only a pure, hungry, seeking heart will ever recline on the furnishings of healing.

If Christians aren't careful, they will find that they have allowed themselves to carry possessions of that "old man," or old nature, back into their hearts.

Don't defend yourself by saying, "The devil bullied me into it. He made me do it!" If the devil had that much power, he would never have allowed you to receive Jesus as your Savior. You have a will. Use it against the devil!

This house of provision Jesus gives is yours! John 15:7 states, "If ye abide in me, and my words abide in you, ye shall ask what ye will, and it shall be done unto you." There *is* an abiding place, and it's in Jesus!

In Him is healing. In Him is health. In Him is joy. In

Him is peace. In Him is love. In Him is prosperity. It's all in Jesus: He is this house of provision!

Enter into Jesus' healing house. Proverbs 18:10 says, "The name of the Lord is a strong tower: the righteous runneth into it, and is safe."

In Jesus is all you'll ever need. Don't go digging around in the dumpster of the past to drag out something to live on, for the past has no life in it. Leave the past under the blood of Jesus. The life is in the blood! Live in Jesus, conscious of His delivering, life-giving blood, and you'll have all the life you'll ever need.

One of my favorite verses is Acts 17:28: "For in him we live, and move, and have our being...." Learn not to make a move unless it moves you into Him!

Bullets of Unbelief

At a time when symptoms of sickness were in my body, the devil was trying to torment my mind with fearful thoughts. Have you ever experienced this kind of spiritual torment?

The Word of God calls Satan "the deceiver." We know that the devil makes his strongest attacks by speaking to our minds. This is the most successful device he uses against most believers. He tries to deceive us into thinking about our situation in a way that is contrary to what the Word of God says. Thus, in order to use his deceptive powers to defeat us, the devil must speak to our mind to deceive it. If he can deceive our thinking, we will not stop him from operating in our life.

This is the strategy the devil used against me when I was standing for my healing. He spoke words to my mind so fast it was as if they were being shot into me by a machine gun. Of course, they were bullets of unbelief!

I've learned that whenever the devil attacks, he sends unbelief with the attack to make you think you don't have an ounce of faith in your heart. Resist that unbelief, which is of the devil, and it will go! Then you'll be free to operate in faith against that attack of the enemy.

The devil will always attack your faith when you're going through a test or a trial. Jesus knew this. He told Peter that Satan desired to have him to sift him as wheat; but Jesus added that He had prayed for Peter so his faith wouldn't fail.

As you resist that attack of unbelief, faith will once again prevail in your heart, and you will rise above the test and trial.

The Holy Spirit Will Come to Your Aid

During my trial of faith, the enemy was saying to my mind, "You'll *never* get better. Just look at other people who have had the same symptoms. They've been that way for *years,* and you will be, too!"

But thank God, when the enemy tries to invade your life, the Spirit of the Lord will raise up a standard against him. If you will follow the Spirit of the Lord at that time, He will guide you out of that situation the enemy is trying to put you in. That's one of the jobs of the Holy Spirit.

Jesus said in reference to the Holy Spirit in John 16:13, "...he will guide you into all truth...." Truth is the Word of God, and the Word of God is victory. Therefore, the Holy Spirit will guide you into victory.

Notice, however, that Jesus did not say that the Holy Spirit would drag or push you into truth. You must *follow* Him willingly, for He is our Guide.

Looking Unto Jesus

The devil was trying to make me look at other people's conditions instead of looking at what the Word said about *my* physical condition.

The devil's aim, of course, is always to take your gaze from Jesus. But Hebrews 12:2 says, "Looking unto Jesus the author and finisher of our faith...."

Lilian B. Yeomans states this so masterfully in one of her books on healing when she calls it "life for a look." I love that. One look at Jesus and that's all it takes!

As I was casting down those thoughts of the enemy, the Holy Spirit spoke so wonderfully and reassuringly to my heart and asked me, "Do you look in your neighbor's checkbook to see if you can pay your bills?"

"Well, no," I exclaimed.

"Then why do you look at someone else's body to see whether or not Jesus has healed you?"

This response of the Holy Spirit smarted a little bit, but I gratefully took the hint, and I'm so glad to report I was wonderfully set free by God's power.

Never let the devil deceive your gaze of faith. Greater is He that is in you than he that is in the world!

When Your Furnace Gets Fiery

Having preached from the Old Testament Book of Daniel about Shadrach, Meshach and Abednego, I'm impressed by their fellowship with God.

Thinking on these scriptures, I've tried to envision what it must have been like at this time in the lives of these three men.

You need to read the third chapter of Daniel to refresh

your memory about this story. Nebuchadnezzar had just built an image of gold and gathered all the leaders of the land together to worship it.

Shadrach, Meshach and Abednego were among the gathering that day, but being God's men, they refused to worship the idol and become the devil's men.

When they wouldn't bow down to Nebuchadnezzar's idol, he had them thrown into a furnace that was heated seven times hotter than it had ever been heated before.

Before being thrown into this fiery furnace, the three Hebrews told the king that their God would deliver them. Think about that!

I wonder how many other people they had seen thrown into that furnace? I'm sure they had seen many. This was the punishment meted out to those who had been sentenced to death.

And I wonder how many times Shadrach, Meshach and Abednego had seen people walk out of the furnace? How many times had Daniel seen people walk out of the lions' den? How many times had Moses seen the Red Sea part? None, none, none on all three accounts!

Faith's Creative Ability

People with faith will believe that God will do something for them, even if they have never seen God do it for anyone else!

Didn't God love others enough to do it for them? Of course He did -- but *they didn't believe He would.*

It doesn't matter if you've never seen God do for someone else what you need Him to do for you. Faith doesn't stop at what God has done for someone else. Faith goes on further to the answer.

The second chapter of Mark relates the story of a man who tried to get into a house where Jesus was ministering.

He was a crippled man who was confined to a bed.

The men carrying him were unable to gain entry through the door because of the crowd, so they carried him up on the roof, tore the roof apart, and let him down right at Jesus' feet. Of course, the man was healed. There was a Healer in that house.

I want you to see that real Bible faith doesn't stop at opposition; it just *bypasses* it.

Bible faith doesn't wait for the door to open upon God's provision. *Bible faith will make its own entrance into the provisions of God.*

If you're waiting for the door of healing or whatever else you need from God to open automatically, Satan will block the door. God's provision is there for the taking, just as these men took what they wanted: healing for their friend.

The wonderful thing is, that's when you please Jesus the most — in **taking** what He has provided for you!

The Roots of Guerilla Warfare

Throughout history, there have been numerous examples of nations at war with one another. Usually, one nation fights for freedom and liberty, while its enemy tries to force an oppressive form of government on it to rule it.

At times the United States has sent troops into foreign lands to lend military support to the nation struggling for its freedom.

After victory has been declared, the U.S. military forces return home, usually leaving some troops in that foreign country to help enforce its victory.

Because defeated nations usually lose the majority of their military weapons, they no longer have the power to continue to engage in a full-blown war.

However, as a desperate last attempt, defeated nations may begin to engage in guerilla warfare. They terrorize the winning nation by placing bombs in public places, on aircraft, and so forth. By killing innocent people and wreaking havoc, they are still making themselves heard.

This is exactly the kind of warfare Satan and his hordes are engaged in against the Body of Christ!

Jesus Freed the Human Race

Realize that Jesus was sent to earth from the "nation" of heaven. He took on the cause of the human race, which was to regain our freedom and liberty from Satan's dominion.

Jesus defeated Satan on his own territory, and rose from the dead victorious.

And in Revelation 1:18, Jesus states, "I...have the keys of hell and of death." Hallelujah! Where did He get them from? He took them from Satan! The Victor always spoils the enemy.

Jesus has won the victory! He has set us free from the bondage of Satan!

Colossians 1:13 declares, "[God] hath delivered us from the power of darkness, and hath translated us into the kingdom of his dear Son."

Colossians 2:15 says, "And having spoiled principalities and powers, he made a shew [show] of them openly, triumphing over them in it."

When the Bible says that Jesus "spoiled" them, it means He took away not only the enemy's power, but also his possessions.

Death no longer has the victory.

Upon defeating the devil, Jesus then returned to His

"nation," heaven. Just as U.S. military troops don't fully abandon the field of victory, but leave troops behind to enforce the victory, Jesus did not leave us abandoned.

Heaven sent its' greatest power, the Holy Spirit, to help us enforce our victory!

The devil hates the fact that he was defeated, so he launches guerilla warfare on believers to make us think that the war is still going on. But it isn't! He no longer has the power to engage in a full-blown war. He has been stripped of his power, to harm and destroy those who trust in God.

Jesus has won the victory for us, and now we must enforce our victory and hold the enemy to it.

Why Satan Plants Bombs in Your Life

Satan's power was spoiled by Jesus. Although Satan no longer has authority over you, he wants you to *think* he does, so he plants "bombs" all around you.

He may plant one in your finances, in your marriage, in your body, or in your job — but you have heaven's "Enforcer," the Holy Spirit, who will show you things to come and will expose Satan's plans!

He may speak to you, telling you that Satan has a plan to attack your finances. You can then enforce your victory with the Word of God, taking authority over the devil and all his devices. In other words, the Holy Spirit will detect the devil's "bombs" and let you know where they are. Then you, in turn, can defuse the bombs by speaking the Word of God to those situations, and by binding the power of the enemy, enforcing your God-given authority! You do all this even before the enemy's plan materializes!

You are the head and not the tail. The Holy Spirit will keep you *in front* of the enemy, not behind him, chasing him around, cleaning up the havoc he has wrought in your life.

The greatest Helper you'll ever have is the Holy Spirit. Learn to work with Him in every area of life.

Satan will launch guerilla warfare attacks on you to try to get you to engage in war again, but don't be deceived: These are just his frantic, desperate, last-ditch attempts to defeat you. The war is over!

Enforce your victory by the Word of God!

There's a Healer in our house!

Introduction

Is God Glorified in Sickness?

Is God glorified in sickness?

We need to know the answer to this question, because *man's tradition* teaches that some people are supposed to be sick so God will be glorified. That's a lie from the pit of hell!

The Bible says if you're a disciple taught by the Lord, you will be taught by the Word of God, not by man. Praise the Lord, I'm not a disciple of a man; I'm a disciple of the Lord Jesus Christ. How do you grow as a disciple of the Lord? By being a student taught by the Word of God.

As my neighbor once pointed out, religion today paints a bad picture of God the Father. Religion says that God *allows* sickness to come on people because He has a purpose in mind to use their sickness. In times past, it was said that God *made* people sick to teach them something.

If God *allows* sickness, as we've been taught, it would be the same as standing by and doing nothing as a truck races toward your child as they cross the street.

There is enough time for you to reach them and snatch them out of harm's way, but, instead, you just stand there and allow them to be run over. "That'll teach them to stay out of the street next time," you say.

You won't have a child for long if that's the way you treat them! Yet that's how some people say God treats His children! They say He allows bad things to happen to His children so they'll learn needed lessons. And many people believe these lies.

The Lord once spoke to me in my spirit and said, "Son, anytime anyone says I do bad things to you, those are demon-inspired words."

Why? Because such statements call God a liar to His face. They say that His Word is not true. This is why religion, or tradition, is so double-minded in the area of healing.

Is Everything God's Will?

Throughout the history of the Church, many erroneous ideas have been taught. One such error is the teaching that everything that happens in the earth is God's will, or He wouldn't let it happen.

God has the *power* to stop or change anything that happens, but He doesn't always have the *right* to do so. I realize this is a very strong statement, so I want to explain it from the Bible.

When God created the earth and placed Adam here, He gave Adam complete dominion over the earth (Genesis 1:28). That dominion belonged to Adam. God didn't say, "Use this dominion for a while until I want it back." No, He said, "Have dominion."

When Adam and Eve submitted to Satan by obeying him, they transferred this dominion into his hands. They changed gods and came under Satan's authority.

We have proof of this in the New Testament, when Jesus was being tempted by Satan. Luke 4:5,6 says:

> **And the devil, taking him up into an high mountain, shewed unto him all the kingdoms of the world in a moment of time.**
>
> **And the devil said unto him, All this power**

> **will I give thee, and the glory of them: for that is
> delivered unto me; and to whomsoever I will give
> it.**

If Satan had been lying about this authority being
delivered to him, Jesus would have corrected him with a
scripture, but He didn't. Satan went on to say in verses 7
and 8:

> **If thou therefore wilt worship me, all shall be
> thine.**

> **And Jesus answered and said unto him, Get
> thee behind me, Satan: for it is written, Thou shalt
> worship the Lord thy God, and him only shalt thou
> serve.**

Another scripture that proves Satan's authority in this
world is Second Corinthians 4:4, where Paul calls Satan
"the god of this world."

The Church's Power

When Jesus came and took our place on Calvary and
went to hell in our place, He stripped Satan of the authority he took from Adam and gave it to His Church.

The problem has been that most of us didn't know we
could use the Name of Jesus and change things in the
earth! Matthew 18:18 says that whatsoever we bind on
earth is bound in heaven.

*God has given us the very same power He used when He
raised Jesus from the dead!* (See Ephesians 1:18-23.) And He
has given us His Word to tell us how to use that power.

*If we don't get in the Word to find out how to use that power
against the devil, God has no choice but to stand by and watch
when bad things happen on the earth, or when His children get
sick.*

But don't get the idea that anytime a Christian gets sick

or has some symptoms, he has sinned, is not reading the Bible, or is not standing on God's promises.

Peter said that Satan roams about like a roaring lion, seeking whom he may devour. Perhaps he roamed around this Christian and attacked him with sickness to see if he might devour him.

A Christian has the choice either to resist the devil by standing on God's Word, or to lie down under the attack and be sick — and even die.

We shouldn't be judging each other anyway. When we see someone who is under Satan's attack, we should begin to apply our faith to his situation. We're all in this together, because we are all members of one body.

God Doesn't Use the Devil's Tools

God does not use the devil's tools to discipline His children, or to get glory. Second Timothy 3:16 says that God's Word — not Satan — is given to teach and correct us! The Holy Spirit is the Teacher whom God sent to us. He doesn't need the devil to accomplish His work.

God is not the author of sickness, tragedies, or tribulations, but we will learn from them. We'll know better next time how to avoid the devil's pitfall, plus we'll be able to help others in their times of need.

Remember the example we gave of a child running out into the street? You wouldn't *plan* to let them get run over and then stand by and watch it happen.

If they had a close call, however, you would take the opportunity to teach them how to cross the street safely and remind them that if they had listened to you in the first place, their close call wouldn't have happened.

What Does God's Word Say?

In the area of healing, we need to know who it is that is causing the problems in our body. *Sickness is not caused by God; it is caused by Satan!* I'm going to prove this to you from the scriptures, because the Bible says, "In the mouth of two or three witnesses shall every word be established" (2 Corinthians 13:1).

John 10:10 is a key scripture in understanding the nature of God. It says, *"The thief* cometh not, but for to steal, and to kill, and to destroy...."

Did I quote that correctly? Doesn't it really say, *"God* cometh not, but for to steal, and to kill, and to destroy"? Does it say that? No!

What does it say? "The thief...." Who's "the thief"? *Satan is the thief!*

The entire verse says, "The thief cometh not, but for to steal, and to kill, and to destroy: I am come that they might have life, and that they might have it more abundantly."

That's Jesus talking! He wants you to have an *abundant, abundant, abundant* life. God never takes anything away from you; He wants you to be blessed abundantly. He wants you to have an abundant life.

Jesus also said, "He that hath seen me hath seen the Father." If you want to see the Father, look at Jesus. They have the same nature. They respond to faith.

If you want to see God in action, read about Jesus' ministry in the following chapters. You can't find any-where in the Word of God where Jesus turned anyone away who wanted to be healed!

Chapter 1

Healing Trends

I would like to share some things about healing trends in the Church and modern society that the Lord laid on my heart during my last trip to Israel.

On this trip, He showed me important facts about healing. I present these facts to you without any apology whatsoever. What I will be teaching will make religious devils nervous, because I'm going to step on tradition.

We were in the ancient city of Capernaum, in the Galilee region, when God began to deal with me about healing in the modern Church.

The Sea of Galilee is one of my favorite spots in Israel. I love it. Like most tour groups, we boarded four or five boats and for a time drifted peacefully on the Sea of Galilee. As we began praising God, the power of God fell.

It's so beautiful by the sea. One reason why I like it so much is because Jesus did 80 percent of His healings in the cities and towns around that region.

Seeking Relief in Worldly Pools

Our guide told us there are many hot springs in Capernaum. During Jesus' day, thousands of people went there for relief from their pains and diseases. Then Jesus would come along, they would look to Him for help, and they would receive their healing.

In Capernaum, tourists visit the ruins of an old synagogue that was built on the foundation of the synagogue

1

Jesus had visited. Peter's house is nearby.

While we were in that old synagogue we praised and worshipped God. Then our leader said, "This spot is where Jesus did a lot of His healings and a lot of miracles." He asked for some short healing testimonies.

One person said, "I got healed of cancer. The Spirit of God came on me, and the tumor disappeared." Another said, "I had bone cancer, and the power of God hit me and I was healed in such-and-such a meeting." And everyone raised their hands and praised the Lord.

Then someone else told how God healed their ankle. And it went on and on. Another person said, "I was ready to die, and God gave me a new heart." We were so happy about all these healings, we lifted our hands and rejoiced every time another testimony was given.

Religion Quenches the Spirit

Suddenly, one of the priests who was an overseer of this synagogue burst through a door in the ruins and yelled, "Shut up!" He was so mad, he was as red as a beet. "Shhh, shhh, shhh! Shut up!" he exclaimed. *"This place is holy!"*

I was so surprised, I almost fell off my seat. I looked around at the rubble (understanding its historical importance), and said, "Man it's just a pile of stones!"

Then God said to me, *"That's what is happening in your churches. My Church has shut up concerning divine healing. They have substituted doctors for divine healing."*

There are all kinds of ways to shut you up about healing and other supernatural works of God. (False doctrine is one thing that can shut you up.)

This experience in Israel took me back in time to an experience I'd once had with another clergyman — a Full

2

Gospel pastor. *My* Full Gospel pastor. ("Full Gospel" means they're supposed to believe the whole Bible.)

I can remember it just like it was yesterday. I was a young believer, and I had gotten hold of healing books by T. L. Osborn and other great men of God and healing tapes by Kenneth Copeland. I got so full of the Word of God that one day my pastor called me into his office for a little conference. *I can relate!*

Carried Away With Healing

He said, "Now, Ed, don't get too carried away with that healing business. Years ago, down in Texas, I pastored a church, and a certain teacher whose materials I know you've been reading came to my church.

"I had a knot on my arm. We were eating lunch after one of the day services, and this man said, 'Brother, why don't you just curse that knot?'

"'Oh, no, no, no. I'll go to the doctor and have it taken off,' I told him.

"'Why don't you just speak to it?'

"'Oh, no, no, no, that's all right.'

"He said, 'Well, would you let *me* speak to it?'

"'Yeah, go ahead.'

"After dinner, he said, 'I curse that thing, and I command it to die!'

"The knot just disappeared."

My pastor told me that story. Then he said, "Don't get mixed up with that healing stuff." In essence, he said, "Shhh!" to healing. Five of his relatives have died since then.

The last time the elders of that church came over to

3

pray for one of my kids, I threw them out.

As usual, they took a little bottle of anointing oil out of their pocket, put a dab on their finger, and made a little cross on the forehead of the sick child, and said, "Now, Lord, if it be thy will..."

But I had learned better by then. I said, "*Stop!* It *is* God's will for that baby to be healed. Now pray right."

"Oh, no, Brother Ed. The pastor told us you were getting into some false stuff."

Jesus Ministers Healing

In Luke 13:10-13 we find how Jesus faced the same kind of opposition from spiritual leaders when He ministered healing to people.

> And he was teaching in one of the synagogues on the sabbath.
>
> And, behold, there was a woman which had a spirit of infirmity eighteen years, and was bowed together, and could in no wise lift up herself.
>
> And when Jesus saw her, he called her to him, and said unto her, Woman, thou art loosed from thine infirmity.
>
> And he laid his hands on her; and immediately she was made straight, and glorified God.

Some people seem to think we should read this another way: "And when Jesus saw her, he called her to him, and said unto her, Woman, you need to keep this infirmity a while longer to teach you something."

It makes people who are bound by traditions of men furious to know the truth that God *wants* to heal people. It made this bunch mad, too. *They didn't recognize that the Healer was in their house of worship that day!*

What About Poor Old Job?

In the Old Testament, man didn't always have the right image of God. That's why Job blamed God. He said, "...the thing which I greatly feared is come upon me" (Job 3:25). In other words, the thing that Job feared happened to him!

Fear activates Satan.

Faith activates God.

People ask, "What about Job? What about poor old Job?"

Job was operating in fear — that's what happened to poor old Job! God didn't afflict him in any way. In fact, God is the One who delivered him.

We saw in verses 12 and 13 that Jesus said, "Woman, thou art loosed from thine infirmity. And He laid his hands on her: and immediately she was made straight, and glorified God."

Notice the woman did not glorify God *before* she was healed, and she did not glorify God for the sickness. She gave God the glory *after* her healing.

I want to show you through scriptures that *nowhere in the New Testament did anyone glorify God for their sickness!* As we saw in this account, God got the glory after this woman was healed. That's when God gets all the glory — for the healing, not for the sickness.

After the woman glorified God for her healing, the story continues in verse 14, "And the ruler of the synagogue answered with indignation, because that Jesus had healed on the sabbath day."

People back then were no different from people today. A lot of people today get madder than a hornet if you tell them God didn't make them sick.

The people in the synagogue were angry because Jesus had healed the woman on the Sabbath day, when no one was supposed to do any work. They were spiritually blinded and ruled by their five senses.

If He had come into their midst and said to the woman, "Now, Sister, because of your sins, you're going to be sick a while longer," they would have said, "Oh, isn't He a great prophet!" But Jesus did good; He healed the woman. The Healer was in their house of worship!

Jesus Stands on the Covenant

The leader of the synagogue said to Jesus, "There are six days in which men ought to work: in them therefore come and be healed, and not on the sabbath day" (verse 14).

Man always makes rules! But you can't put the Holy Spirit in a box.

This is how the Lord answered the man (verses 15 and 16):

> Thou hypocrite, doth not each one of you on the sabbath loose his ox or his ass from the stall, and lead him away to watering?
>
> And ought not this woman, being a daughter of Abraham, whom Satan hath bound, lo, these eighteen years, be loosed from this bond on the sabbath day?

Who had bound this woman? God?

Jesus said Satan had bound her! Furthermore, Jesus pointed out that she was a daughter of Abraham. Are you of the seed of Abraham? According to Galatians 3:27-29, every born-again believer is of the seed of Abraham!

Jesus understood the Abrahamic covenant, but those people — even the leader of the synagogue — didn't know their covenant, and didn't know when the Healer was in their house.

The passage continues: "And when he had said these things, all his adversaries were ashamed: and all the people rejoiced for all the glorious things that were done by him" (verse 17).

God got glory for the *healing;* He didn't get praise for the *sickness.* The oppressor was Satan; the Deliverer was Jesus. Jesus said so.

The State of the Modern Church

Notice the same devil that fights healing that was in the synagogue two thousand years ago is still hanging around in our churches — today!

Today Christians are getting bigger church buildings. We're getting stained glass windows. We're on the other side of the tracks. The mayor is talking to us now. Forty-five minutes of teaching. Run them in. Run them out. Be dignified. Yes, we must not get too loud.

I want you to know there was *noise* on the Day of Pentecost! No one was going around whispering, "Shhh, shhh! This is holy!" I'm sick of preachers saying "Shhh" over a bunch of dumb rocks.

"Oh, that altar's holy. Grandma's tears from 1907 are on that bench. Shhh! Don't let that dirty hippie come down here and pray. Shhh!"

We'd better watch out about trying to get dignified! What my Savior provided for me on Calvary makes me want to dance, glory to God!

It would do some of you dignified people good to run around the church. I was in a brand new church one night, and the power of God hit me. God said, "Run across the pews." I took off across those new pews. It had to have been supernatural, for I hit every one of them without falling.

The people didn't laugh. They were upset because I had stepped on their new pews. I like what one pastor told his congregation. He said, "We're going to have beautiful pews, but, I'm warning you, if you sit down on your faith, I'm jerking every one of those pews out and putting hard chairs in here."

There are always those who say, "I want something *deep.*"

What Jesus provided for you on Calvary is deep.

Our churches are filled with people like that who cruise from church to church. They never get involved or committed. They follow "lights," "smoke," and such, running here and there in search of the presumed supernatural.

"Oh, Dr. Light is over here. I'm going over here."

"Oh, the Smoke Man's coming to town. I'm going over there and get my healing tonight."

They're running from this "hot spring" to that "hot spring," trying to get relief, because they don't want to tear themselves away from their television set, get in the Word of God, and discern what Jesus provided for us at Calvary.

It's time to grow up! If you're just playing games and you're not in the Word of God, you're going to get trampled and run over.

God dealt with me about what's going to happen in America in this next revival.

I predict that churches will arise across America that will know how to discern the Lord's Body and know how to pray for the sick. They will stand up and declare that the healing power of God is for you and me today.

They're not going to say "Shhh" in reaction to healing; they're going to let the power of the living God flow in their services, and they're going to empty out the hospitals! Yes, they're going to empty out the hospitals.

Today, instead of flocking to springs, people are flocking to ungodly hospitals for relief. Why aren't they coming to the Church for healing? Because we haven't really believed the healing message. We really *don't* believe that God will heal today.

When they're in pain, believers reach for the pill bottle instead of the Bible. If you ask them why, they'll tell you, "That way I don't have to believe."

If they're suffering from something more serious, many believers say, "Well, I'll let Brother So-and-so pray for me, but if it doesn't work, I've got my health insurance to fall back on."

I'm not against doctors, medicine, or insurance, but we need to learn to depend on Jesus and feed our faith. That's what God spoke to me about at Capernaum. He said, "People were all around these hot springs, trying to get relief, and that's what people are still doing today."

But I predict it won't be long until you see the Church of the '90s rise up with healing power and the working of miracles. You'll see wheelchairs lined up in the churches, and you'll see ambulances backing up to the church doors.

And the devil of greed is going to be so mad, hospitals will sue the churches that are preaching healing. "You're practicing medicine without a license," they'll charge.

I also predict that in the '90s, most secular television stations are going to say, "Shhh! We don't want any of that healing stuff." Some are already starting to make such policies. This attitude is already taking root even in some of our Christian stations. "Now, don't get too wild. Just keep it nice. We don't want to show you saying, 'Come out, in the Name of Jesus!' Someone might have a heart attack. You might offend other people." That's religious devils.

History's Greatest Healing Revival Is Ahead

We're right on the verge of the greatest healing revival this world has ever seen!

The next few years will be critical. History proves that there have always been parts of the Church of Jesus Christ that have missed every wave of God.

We must get in the right position for God to move in our lives and our churches. We must determine in our hearts that we won't miss God. We must want the perfect will of God for our lives.

This is what I want for my life and ministry. God has said to me, "Son, one of your responsibilities is to tell the truth concerning a healing Jesus."

Why do you think the devil is fighting the Church so much, and is trying to destroy the people of God? He has tried to stop men of God, but he hasn't been too successful.

The devil is having a nervous breakdown over the ones who will not compromise the Word of God — the ones who will stand up and proclaim, "We believe in the healing Jesus!"

There was a healing Jesus two thousand years ago who went around the cities and towns of Galilee and healed the sick and set them free.

That healing Jesus is still alive today! He still heals today! He still brings people out of wheelchairs. He knows how to put in new livers, new hearts, and new eyeballs.

There's still a Healer in the house!

Chapter 2

Jesus' Ministry
Expresses God's Will

Luke 18:35 tells us, "And it came to pass, that as he was come nigh unto Jericho, a certain blind man sat by the way side begging."

I was meditating on this story one day, and God showed me in my spirit, like a movie, the whole thing that took place. I saw the blind man. I know what he looked like. When I get to heaven, you won't have to tell me who he is, because as soon as I see him, I'll recognize him.

> And hearing the multitude pass by, he asked what it meant.
>
> And they told him, that Jesus of Nazareth passeth by.
>
> And he cried, saying, Jesus, thou son of David, have mercy [compassion] on me.
>
> And they which went before rebuked him, that he should hold his peace: but he cried so much the more, Thou son of David, have mercy on me.
>
> Luke 18:36-39

The same spirit that was in the synagogue was present that day, telling the blind man, "Shhh! Shut up!" Jesus' own disciples said, "Don't you know who this man is? This is holy!"

A translation of this story from Mark 10:48,49 reads, "Shut up! some of the people yelled at him. But he only shouted the louder, again and again, O Son of David, have

11

mercy on me!"

Blind Bartimaeus didn't care about the multitude that surrounded Jesus. He didn't care what tradition thought. He didn't care what anyone thought. He knew the Healer was present that day along that dusty road, and all he wanted was to receive his sight.

Faith Brings Jesus on the Scene

He called out, "Thou son of David, have mercy on me!" And Jesus stopped in His tracks.

The morning I was meditating on this passage, I saw Jesus stop, turn around, and tell the multitudes, "Get out of my way!" He started walking over to the blind man. That man's faith *drew* Jesus. His faith *stopped* Jesus!

You've got to realize this blind man wasn't living under the New Covenant, as we are, so *if his faith stopped Jesus, yours will, too!*

Smith Wigglesworth said, "When you use your faith, Jesus will pass over a million people just to get to you."

If blind Bartimaeus had shut up the first time someone asked him to, Jesus would have kept on walking. Today, there are a lot of Christians who are shutting up about healing.

But I want you to know that God has never changed, and His Word has never changed. He is the same yesterday, and today, and forever. If God says it's His will for you to be healed, then it's His will for you to be healed.

A Change of Attitude

Verse 40 says, "And Jesus stood, and commanded him to be brought unto him..."

The people who were with Jesus changed their attitude

about the blind man in a hurry when Jesus sent for him. Even the crowd probably thought, "This man is a friend of Jesus; we'd better get close to him." One translation states, "'You lucky fellow,' they said, 'come on, he's calling you.'"

People might laugh and tell you to shut up or talk about you when you're using your faith, but when they see it working, they'll say, "Oh, you lucky fellow! We're going to get involved with you."

I'm a friend of Jesus. I'm a son of God. Jesus and I are together all the time. When I'm sleeping, He's still there, because the Holy Spirit is inside me. I'm wall-to-wall Holy Ghost — and so are you, if you've been born again! He's right on the inside of you.

Just speak the Word of God, my friend, for your healing, believe it in your heart, and it will come to pass! There's a Healer in your house!

Jesus asked the blind man, "What wilt thou that I shall do unto thee? And he said, Lord, that I may receive my sight" (verse 41).

Notice Jesus' reply. Did He say harshly, "Because you gave my disciples a hard time, you're going to keep that blindness another 24 hours, until you become a better person"? No.

The reason I'm bringing this up is so you'll catch it when tradition says things like that. It will ring a bell in your spirit. You'll say, "No, that isn't right."

"Thy Faith Hath Saved Thee"

This is what actually happened: "And Jesus said unto him, Receive thy sight: thy faith hath saved thee" (verse 42). "Saved" in the Greek means healing and prosperity. Some people today teach, "Healing passed away with the disciples." But it did not pass away.

Jesus said, "Thy faith hath saved thee." What? *"Thy faith — thy faith — thy faith!"* And faith hasn't passed away! Since the blind man was healed by faith, you can be healed by faith.

Jesus didn't say, "Just because you yelled loud, I'm going to heal you. Just because I like the way you look, the way you comb your hair, and the way you believe in your denomination, I'm going to heal you." No! He said, "Thy *faith* hath saved thee."

The blind beggar's faith drew out the healing anointing on Jesus' life!

"And immediately he received his sight, and followed him, glorifying God..." (verse 43).

I like people who won't give up their faith. I love this man. In fact, I can hardly wait to get to heaven just to hug him and say, "Praise God for your faith. I read in the Bible what you did, and I learned that I could do the same thing!"

The story ends, "...and all the people, when they saw it, *gave praise unto God."*

Does God get glorified through sickness? No! God is a good God.

There's A Healer in the House!

The second chapter of Mark reveals one of the times Jesus exercised His authority.

> **And again he entered into Capernaum after some days; and it was noised that he was in the house.**
>
> **And straightway many were gathered together, insomuch that there was no room to receive them, no, not so much as about the door: and he preached the word unto them.**

And they come unto him, bringing one sick of the palsy, which was borne of four.

And when they could not come nigh unto him for the press, they uncovered the roof where he was: and when they had broken it up, they let down the bed wherein the sick of the palsy lay.

When Jesus saw their faith, he said unto the sick of the palsy, Son, thy sins be forgiven thee.

But there were certain of the scribes sitting there, and reasoning in their hearts,

Why doth this man thus speak blasphemies? who can forgive sins but God only?

And immediately when Jesus perceived in his spirit that they so reasoned within themselves, he said unto them, Why reason ye these things in your hearts?

Whether is it easier to say to the sick of the palsy, Thy sins be forgiven thee; or to say, Arise, and take up thy bed, and walk?

But that ye may know that the Son of man hath power on earth to forgive sins, (he saith to the sick of the palsy,)

I say unto thee, Arise, and take up thy bed, and go thy way into thine house.

And immediately he arose, took up the bed, and went forth before them all; insomuch that they were all amazed, and glorified God, saying, We never saw it on this fashion.

And he went forth again by the sea side: and all the multitude resorted unto him, and he taught them.

Mark 2:1-13

Notice the multitude didn't glorify God over this man's sickness. They didn't exclaim, "Oh, praise God for this sickness! Oh, we thank You, God, that he's going to keep it another 10 years, just to become humble and spiritual."

No! Something in their heart told them that Jesus was a good man. The attitude of the man's friends was, "We must get our friend with the palsy to Jesus, for He will heal him." They literally tore the house apart to get him to Jesus!

They knew there was a Healer in that house!

Someone had preached to them and put a good image of the heavenly Father into their hearts.

The Woman Whose Money Ran Out

Do you remember the story in Mark 5 about the woman with the issue of blood? Someone had preached the Gospel to her, too. Someone had told her that Jesus was doing good things, because verse 27 tells us she had heard of Jesus.

> **And a certain woman, which had an issue of blood twelve years,**
>
> **And had suffered many things of many physicians, and had spent all that she had, and was nothing bettered, but rather grew worse,**
>
> **When she had heard of Jesus, came in the press behind, and touched his garment.**
>
> **For she said, If I may touch but his clothes, I shall be whole.**
>
> **Mark 5:25-28**

I was reading this one day, and God dealt with me. He said, "Son, she'd been sick for 12 years. She was a very wealthy woman, because it took her 12 years before she spent all her money. That's a lot of money."

After she spent everything she had, she heard that

Jesus was coming. We must understand that people living under the Old Testament, as she was, knew that prophets had healing anointing in their mantles. She knew that. It's a shame she had to wait until she spent everything that she had.

This woman spent everything, and it took 12 years. Then she heard of a prophet coming through town. She got back to her beliefs. "The prophet of God has the healing anointing," she thought. That's why she said, "If I may touch his mantle, I shall be healed."

Notice what she said in verse 28: "If I may touch but his clothes, I shall be whole." Another translation says, "And when she heard of Jesus, she came in the press behind, and touched his mantle. For she said, If I may touch his mantle, I shall be whole."

The Shunammite Who Sought the Anointing

Remember the Shunammite woman whose young son suddenly died? She sought out Elisha, the prophet of God, who had prophesied that she would have this child (2 Kings 4:8-37). Elisha first sent his servant with his staff, but the child was not raised.

The Shunammite woman said, "I don't want your staff. I want you — I want the anointing that's on you — to heal my child." She made him come to her house.

When the prophet stretched his body across the dead child's, the boy was raised from the dead. Yes, the anointing was in Elisha's clothing, but it was also on the "mantle" that was on his life.

You must realize that the woman with the issue of blood did have faith, because if people had realized what she, a woman in an unclean condition, was about to do, they would have stoned her.

She was broke. She had become what we call a "bag lady." But she said, "If I may touch his mantle..."

You know the story. Jesus was walking as the Son of God, but He wasn't walking in all the privileges He had in heaven. While on earth, He walked under the Abrahamic covenant and in the gifts of the Spirit.

He asked, "Who touched my clothes?" He didn't even know who touched His clothes, but someone had made a demand on His anointing. He looked around to see who had done this thing, and the woman came to Him, trembling.

The doctors wouldn't have anything more to do with her, because she didn't have any more money.

This will never happen to you, but let's use it as an example. Suppose you get hit by a car, an ambulance comes and takes you to the hospital, and you don't have health insurance or money. What will they do?

They will turn you out.

Coming Judgment on the Medical Profession

I've got a friend who needs a liver transplant, and they won't even *talk* to him unless he has $125,000.

I predict that we're going to start seeing judgment come on the medical profession, because most of it is run by greed. (I know it takes money to operate a business.)

Even though there are good doctors, the simple point I'm making is: *Doctors don't love you as much as God loves you!*

It's a shame that this suffering woman had to have her back against the wall to look to a healing Jesus. Why should we wait until we run out of money and they throw us out of the hospital until we look to a healing Jesus? Why should we wait until we're completely down to the bottom until we look to a healing Jesus? We're going to have to depend on a healing Jesus in this next wave of God.

"Oh, but he's my favorite doctor."

Run out of money and you'll find out how much he loves you. Lose your health insurance, and you'll find out how much he loves you.

You may ask, "Do you believe in doctors?" Let me make a statement here: Most definitely I believe in doctors, but they're not your Healer.

The Body of Christ has almost come to the place where we say, "Doctors are the healers." No, they're not. They can't heal you. They can only clean up a wound. They can only cut something out — but they cannot *heal* you.

We've dropped our faith. We've become complacent. Jesus Christ is the same yesterday, and today, and forever. He was the healing Jesus in Capernaum, and He's still the healing Jesus today.

They didn't have Blue Cross back in Jesus' day. Today people have more faith in their health plan than in the healing power of God. There's nothing wrong, of course, with having a health plan — unless you're depending on the plan for your healing.

Jesus Shows God's Love by Healing

In Matthew 15:29, 30 we have another example of Jesus' healing ministry.

> **And Jesus departed from thence, and came nigh unto the sea of Galilee; and went up into a mountain, and sat down there.**
>
> **And great multitudes came unto him, having with them those that were lame, blind, dumb, maimed, and many others, and cast them down at Jesus' feet....**

19

What happened next? Did Jesus tell these sick people to keep their sickness for a while until they became better people? No!

What does the Bible say? Verse 30 continues, "and he healed them." Who was "them"? The lame, the blind, the dumb, the maimed, and many others. He healed them! The Healer was in their midst!

Then verse 31 relates, "Insomuch that the multitude wondered, when they saw the dumb to speak, the maimed to be whole, the lame to walk, and the blind to see: *and they glorified the God of Israel."*

This makes me want to shout all over the place! *The Amplified Bible* says, "They recognized God." When healings occur in a place, people will recognize God. *They will recognize that there's a Healer in the house.*

That's why many in Kathryn Kuhlman's meetings would turn to God. They recognized God was at work in their midst, and they knew in their hearts that He is a good God. *They recognized that there was a Healer in the house!*

The devil would like to twist the image of the Father and get you discouraged, causing you to think God is doing bad things to you. No, He isn't, because God loves you.

Remember, *God gets glorified in the healing, not in the sickness!* Now that you know the truth, you won't be hoodwinked the next time someone comes along and preaches something different to you.

Jesus Shows God's Love for Outcasts

Luke records an encounter Jesus had with the outcasts of that society — lepers.

> **And it came to pass, as he went to Jerusalem, that he passed through the midst of Samaria and**

Galilee.

And as he entered into a certain village, there met him ten men that were lepers, which stood afar off:

And they lifted up their voices, and said, Jesus, Master, have mercy [compassion] on us.

Luke 17:11-13

What was Jesus' answer? Did He say, "No, I'm not going to heal you today, because you guys have been bad dudes and you need to learn a few things. You keep that leprosy, and after your eyeballs fall out, your ears fall off, your noses fall off, and your legs fall off, I might do something about it, because then you'll be spiritual."

Jesus didn't say that, did He? I know it sounds silly, but a lot of people believe that was His attitude. These people need to get a proper image of their heavenly Father so Satan won't be able to hoodwink them. Then they'll know that God loves them, and they'll understand that they have been made the righteousness of God.

You won't have any trouble with faith if you know you are in right standing with God. You won't have a sense of sin-consciousness when you enter His Throne Room.

Yes, you will miss it sometimes, but when you say, "Father, I sinned today — I got ugly at my brother — will You forgive me," He'll answer, "Yes, you're forgiven according to First John 1:9." And you will hear Him say, "Come on in, son," and you will be able to walk into His presence.

You'll walk out of there and praise God like you had never sinned. He has forgotten it. I realize this sounds rather cocky to the natural man, but our Father loves us.

Faith Brings Healing

Jesus didn't tell the lepers to keep their leprosy. He said, "Go shew yourselves unto the priests..." (verse 14).

There is something important to be seen here. These lepers could have reasoned, "He's telling us to go show ourselves to the priests, but doesn't He realize that if we even approach them, they'll *stone* us?"

Lepers always had to stay "afar off"; they weren't allowed near healthy people. People threw rocks at them if they got too close. No one wanted them.

Jesus was telling them to get up close and show themselves to the priests. These lepers must have heard about Jesus and thought, "If He says it, let's do it!" That's what we should do: Act on the Word of God! Know there's a Healer in the house!

They could have said, "That preacher is nuts. Let's not listen to Him. Let's go back and continue to be unclean." Instead, the lepers started out in faith to visit the priests. At first they didn't see anything; they just acted on the words of Jesus and did what He said. Then the Bible says:

> And it came to pass, that, as they went, they were cleansed.
>
> And one of them, when he saw that he was healed, turned back, and with a loud voice glorified God,
>
> And fell down on his face at his feet, giving him thanks: and he was a Samaritan.
>
> Luke 17:14-16

God got glory in the healing! Notice, too, that one of the lepers glorified God with a *loud* voice. That's what I like about people who get healed: They don't care what anyone thinks. They praise God with a loud voice. Others may talk about them, but so what? They have received their healing!

> And Jesus answering said, Were there not ten cleansed? but where are the nine?
>
> There are not found that returned to give glory to God, save this stranger.
>
> And he said unto him, Arise, go thy way: thy faith hath made thee whole.

Luke 17:17-19

The Power of Praise

I saw something there I hadn't seen before: *There's power in praise!*

The tenth leper came back and gave glory to God for his healing. Some people lose their healing when they say, "I'm not going to praise God, because I've still got the pain." But the leper returned and glorified God for being cleansed of the leprosy.

Jesus said to him, "Thy faith hath made thee *whole.*" What does "whole" mean to a leper? What does leprosy do? It eats away at its victims!

All 10 lepers were *cleansed* of their leprosy. Although the process of the disease was stopped in their bodies, their bodies weren't restored from the effects of the leprosy.

The tenth leper, however, came back praising God, and Jesus said, "Thy faith hath made thee *whole.*" He had body parts and flesh restored because he went a step further than they did: He gave God the glory for his healing.

His fingers and feet were restored, his nose and ears popped back on, his hair returned, and everything else that was missing was replaced. He was made *whole!*

The other lepers got cleansed, but they forgot to give God glory for their healing; although the leprosy process was stopped in their bodies, they were not made whole.

God gets the most glory in your healing, not in the sickness. Sickness is from the pit of hell. Poverty, strife, confusion, unbelief, rebellion, depression, and anything unlike God is from the pit of hell. You must resist these things like you resist sickness.

Know that *there's a Healer in the house!*

Chapter 3

Healing: God's Calling Card

Do you know what God's "calling card" is? People being healed! A person's illness never drew anyone to God.

Romans 8:28 is often quoted: "And we know that all things work together for good to them that love God...." This verse, however, is referring to prayer, not to all the bad things that happen to people.

Your spirit, the Holy Spirit, and all of God's armor listed in Ephesians 6 will work together for good when you're spending time in prayer, praying in tongues and believing God.

When I first started out in my ministry, a man who claimed he was a Bible scholar came to one of my meetings. Although he had already had five years of college, he still didn't have a job.

A man walked into that meeting on crutches but carried them out. He was completely healed. Scars were disappearing. Eyes were being opened. Legs were lengthened.

But the whole time I was praying for the people, this so-called Bible scholar was muttering, "You can't do that! You can't do that! That's not what my Bible school taught."

I said, "I'm doing it."

I didn't even know how to preach at that time. I just brought my tape recorder, set it up, and we listened to tapes by Kenneth E. Hagin, Kenneth Copeland, and others. Afterwards we had a healing service, and I prayed for the sick. That's all I knew.

Then I started repeating a few things our "guest speakers" had said. I was turned on to the Word, and God started giving me some sermons. Finally I started preaching the Word of God myself. Praise God, the anointing is on His Word, and people were saved and healed.

God Receives Glory When We Exercise Our Authority

Now Peter and John went up together into the temple at the hour of prayer, being the ninth hour.

And a certain man lame from his mother's womb was carried, whom they laid daily at the gate of the temple which is called Beautiful, to ask alms of them that entered into the temple.

Acts 3:1, 2

When passersby saw the lame man at the gate, did they all praise God because of his infirmity? No, the reason he was lying at the gate was because he was begging for alms. That was his only means of livelihood.

Who seeing Peter and John about to go into the temple asked an alms.

And Peter, fastening his eyes upon him with John, said, Look on us.

And he gave heed unto them, expecting to receive something of them.

Then Peter said, Silver and gold have I none; but such as I have give I thee: In the name of Jesus Christ of Nazareth rise up and walk.

And he took him by the right hand, and lifted him up: and immediately his feet and ancle bones received strength.

And he leaping up stood, and walked, and entered with them into the temple, walking, and leaping, and praising God.

Acts 3:3-8

God got all the glory for the lame man's healing, not for his sickness. "And all the people saw him walking and praising God" (verse 9).

He praised God and they praised God. They praised God for his healing, not for the fact that he was sick all those years so he could be humble.

The lame man was expecting to receive some money from Peter and John, but he received something far better than money: The power in the Name of Jesus is what Peter and John gave him. They knew the Healer was present to heal this man.

God's power will work the same through any born-again believer as it did through Peter and John at the Gate Beautiful. Jesus gave us His Name and the authority to use it in Mark 16:17,18:

> **And these signs shall follow them that believe; In my name shall they cast out devils; they shall speak with new tongues:**
>
> **They shall take up serpents; and if they drink any deadly thing, it shall not hurt them; they shall lay hands on the sick, and they shall recover.**
>
> If you're a believer, these signs shall follow you!

How Does God Teach His People?

God revealed this message to me one day when a horrible teaching was going around that God was the one who was making people sick in order to teach them things.

Don't get me wrong: You *can* learn things out of sickness, but why should a bit have to be put in your mouth so you can learn something?

What does the Bible say about God's teaching? Isaiah 53 describes prophetically what actually happened when Jesus was on the cross. It teaches that as Jesus became sin

27

for us, and as all our sicknesses were put on Him, His appearance was marred beyond recognition.

Also, the chastisement (meaning punishment by pain) needful to obtain our peace was put on Jesus. He paid the price for our redemption.

Chapter 54 talks about the redeemed. Verse 13 says, "And all thy children shall be taught of the Lord; and great shall be the peace of thy children." Taught of the Lord!

Second Timothy 3:16,17 says, "All scripture is given by inspiration of God, and is profitable for doctrine, for reproof, for correction, for instruction in righteousness: That the man of God may be perfect, thoroughly furnished unto all good works." The Word of God is good for teaching and correcting. If you want to get corrected, get into the epistles. They will clean you up.

Jesus Teaches About Prayer

In Matthew 7, Jesus gave this teaching:

Ask, and it shall be given you; seek, and ye shall find; knock, and it shall be opened unto you:

For every one that asketh receiveth; and he that seeketh findeth; and to him that knocketh it shall be opened.

Or what man is there of you, whom if his son ask bread, will he give him a stone?

Or if he ask a fish, will he give him a serpent?

If ye then, being evil, know how to give good gifts unto your children, how much more shall your Father which is in heaven give good things to them that ask him?

Matthew 7:7-11

What is Jesus doing here? He's trying to paint an image in your spirit. "Ask, and you shall receive," He says. "God is a good God!"

Jesus is teaching about prayer in the sixth and seventh chapters of Matthew. And right in the middle of this teaching, in Matthew 7:15, He says, "Beware of false prophets, which come to you in sheep's clothing, but inwardly they are ravening wolves."

I looked up "ravening wolves" in the Greek and found it means "spoiling lights." What does the word "light" mean? "The revelation of the Word of God."

There are the false prophets going around the earth today, spoiling, or twisting, the revelation of your heavenly Father.

In Matthew 7:7, Jesus is trying to give you a good image of your Father. He says that God won't give you a snake if you ask for a fish. And right in the middle of telling you that God is a good God, Jesus warns you to watch out for false prophets.

People who don't know any better are going around and twisting the revelation of the Father. That's why the Body of Christ has been in such darkness all these years: Christians have had the wrong revelation of our Father in heaven.

God's Will Is Healing

Years ago, there was a Bible student who gave me a bad time in a Bible study. He told the group, "I know someone who didn't get healed."

(What about the ones who did?)

He went on to describe a beautiful young woman lying in a hospital room, dying with a disease. He painted such an appealing scene. He told about the nurses this girl won to the Lord before she died. He said that God had allowed the sickness so she could win those nurses.

"Isn't that wonderful?" he concluded. Some of the people began to weep.

I was preaching the Word of God to them, and here they were, crying over a poor girl who had died five years before, after winning some nurses to the Lord.

God could have healed her, and she could have won 500 people to the Lord and gone home to heaven at 80 years of age! After all, *there's a Healer in the house!*

Why do you have to be *sick* to go to the hospital to witness? Why don't you go there anyway?

If you're sick in a hospital, God will take advantage of the situation and show His love through you to the lost that are there. But that isn't His perfect will for you. He'd rather you win the whole hospital to the Lord *while you're well.*

If sickness is a blessing from God, then my mother was blessed tremendously. She was in and out of institutions most of her life. She was constantly sick.

People try to tell me that *God* did that. I'd rather serve the devil if that were true, but it isn't! It was Satan who did that to her, not my God.

Should You Praise God for Sickness?

You can praise God *in* sickness because the manifestation of your healing is coming — but you shouldn't praise God *for* the sickness.

Do you know what god you're praising when you praise God for sickness? You're praising the god of sickness, who is Satan! You may not know it, but you are.

God is not the god of sickness. He doesn't have any sickness.

Doctrines saying that God wants some people to be

sick come from the pit of hell to make the Christian double-minded. Jesus never turned anyone down who asked
Him for healing. He didn't say, "You must keep your
leprosy for a while." No, He said, "Your faith has made
you whole!"

Jesus' attitude always was and is, *"What can I do for
you? What can I do for you? What can I do for you?"* He never
turns anyone down — but He never forces healing on
anyone, either.

Jesus responds to faith, not to whims. He doesn't
suddenly decide, "I like this fellow. He's good looking,
and he's got a nice moustache. I think I'll heal him of that
cold." The Lord doesn't have any favorites. Although He
put me in a healing ministry, I have to believe Him for my
healing, too.

I woke up one morning with a throbbing headache. It
was still pounding after I got to the office. It would have
been so easy to give in to it and go back home, telling
myself, "I think I'll lie down. No one will miss me. I can
read my Bible in bed. I need a rest anyway; I've been
working too hard."

That's what the devil told me to do. I said, "You're a
liar, devil! Healed men don't lie in bed when they should
be working."

I remained at the office, stood on God's Word that says
I'm healed, and received the manifestation of my healing.

There's a Healer in my house!

The Word: Anointed To Heal

Early in my ministry, a certain man told me, "You
don't pronounce words correctly. You'll have to go to
speech school for 10 years before you can preach." He
almost had me convinced. I almost quit preaching the

Gospel.

Finally I realized that if I'm preaching the Word of God, I don't need to worry about how it comes out, because it's anointed. God will anoint the preaching of His Word.

Promote the Word, and the Word will promote you. I don't care where you are in life — promote the healing Word. If you need healing, promote the Word and you'll be promoted into health.

When the storms of life come your way, act like an eagle. Spread your wings of faith. The wind of the Holy Spirit will pick you up, and you'll soar over all those trials.

That's what an eagle does. When an eagle sees a storm coming, he locks his wings in a flight position. When that big storm comes — sickness, trials, tests — the winds lift him up above it. He can soar thousands of feet high, and he'll stay up there while the storm is blowing, raging, and tearing everything up down below. He just soars above it.

All the chickens down in the chicken coop will be running around looking for someplace to hide while Mr. Eagle soars safely up above the storm. When the storm is over, he comes back down.

Turned on to the Word

I thank God for His Word. After being saved for four years, I said, "Phooey on this religion junk!" I was filled with the Holy Spirit. I was a deacon and greeter in the church. I did everything — I even cleaned the toilets — but I was still unhappy.

The outside of my Bible was worn out, but the inside was brand new. I was a real Bible-toter. I carried it everywhere. I thought that was the right thing to do. "Look, I'm a Christian!" I was proclaiming.

I never got *inside* my Bible until 1971 when I went to Denver, Colorado, and heard Kenneth Copeland preach about the covenant man David. There I heard for the first time that I could stand on God's Word, for it is true.

Don't you dare tell someone to stand on the Word for healing and then tell them it might not be God's will to heal everyone. There *is* a Healer in the house.

Chapter 4

The Benefits of Calvary

And I, brethren, when I came to you, came not with excellency of speech or of wisdom, declaring unto you the testimony of God.

For I determined not to know any thing among you, save Jesus Christ, and him crucified.

1 Corinthians 2:1,2

We need to be determined to say the same thing Paul said here. I would phrase it, "I don't want to hear any gossip. I don't want to hear any tale-bearing. I don't want to know anything except Jesus Christ and Him crucified!"

Another translation says this: "I am determined not to cultivate any other knowledge, or esteem any other doctrine as worthy of notice, save Jesus Christ and *the benefits of the cross.*"

I've been in the ministry more than 27 years, but I still feel like an apprentice. The more you get involved in the ministry, the more you find out the less you know.

Of course, when you start out, you think you know *everything.* You get hold of Mark 11:22 and 23, and you think you know the whole Bible. But there is so much more for us to learn and experience in God!

Divine Discontent

We should never be satisfied with our current spiritual status. I'm certainly not satisfied. I'm not satisfied where I'm at in God, and I'm not satisfied with the results I'm

35

having in my ministry.

I'm having good results, but I'm still not satisfied with them. In fact, I have a sense of divine discontent, and I always want to have it, so I won't get in a spiritual rut and lose out.

Part of my dissatisfaction is because we in the Body of Christ are not really helping people as much as we could. We serve a mighty God, and we appreciate His anointing, but we're not seeing the mighty signs and wonders that the apostles saw in Acts 5:12-16 and elsewhere.

Another reason why it's easy to be dissatisfied is because of all the doctrinal differences we find in today's Church. Is there a Rapture, or isn't there? Is this the kingdom of God, or is it coming later? Should we war in the Spirit or not? All these discussions are going on.

How To Keep Your Doctrine Straight

I was pondering these questions one day, and the Lord began to deal with me about our text, First Corinthians 1:1,2. I've preached from it before, using different approaches.

The Lord said, "Do you know how you can keep your doctrine straight?"

That's when He showed me that phrase, "I don't want to know anything but the cross."

If the cross and the benefits Jesus provided on it aren't involved in preaching, there's no anointing on it. Furthermore, if a doctrine or a ministry isn't in line with the cross of Jesus Christ, it won't last.

Trends in Teaching

The other day I heard a man who is an excellent preacher. I really liked a lot of what he said, but he was trying to prove something in eschatology, the study of the end times.

I didn't agree with everything he said, but it didn't bother me. I didn't get upset and walk out of the meeting, because I've seen these trends come and go.

He was trying to prove that he has end-time prophecy figured out. Unfortunately, the more he tries to push his theories, the more it's going to hurt his ministry and his anointing.

His theories may be popular right now, but they won't last. Have you ever noticed how things in the world get popular? Hula hoops were popular once; today it's skateboards. Tomorrow it will be something else. That's just the way the flesh is: It always has to have something new and different.

I am going to stay with the Word, how about you? I am determined to know nothing but Jesus Christ and Him crucified. I am determined to know nothing but the benefits of Calvary.

Keep Calvary and its benefits in everything you preach, and you'll stay fresh, sharp, and hot for God!

Let's read that other translation again: "I am determined not to cultivate any other knowledge, or esteem any other doctrine as worthy of notice, save Jesus Christ and *the benefits of the cross.*"

Many doctrines are vying for our attention, but we must pass over them and concentrate on the benefits of the cross: the blood and our redemption from sin, sickness, and disease.

What Does Communion Mean?

I'll never forget the night we had a Communion service at the Full Gospel church where I got saved and served as a deacon. It was beautiful. We had candles and everything.

The pastor said, "Now this emblem, the cup, represents the blood, and this emblem, the bread, represents the Lord's body."

I said, "Lord, I really don't understand it."

Most believers don't really understand what it means when they receive Communion. They don't know the benefits of the cross!

How do I know this? Because when we're in Full Gospel churches, most of the congregation always comes forward for prayer for healing! You'll see this scene repeated in most Pentecostal, Full Gospel, and Charismatic churches. The situation has concerned me for many years.

Either we're doing something wrong, or the people just don't understand the benefits of the cross, because *we are the healed! There's a Healer in our house!*

Living Beneath Our Benefits

Healing is supposed to be the "dinner bell" to summon the world to come to church and get saved and healed. Healing has *already* been provided for you and me as believers, so why aren't we healed? What is the problem?

We're not healed because we're not walking in our benefits.

We're not healed because we don't understand there's a Healer in the house!

If you have insurance on your car, you're in a wreck, and then you pay for it to be fixed, that isn't very smart. It's already covered if you have a policy with collision benefits, and you need only to pay the deduction. Walk in your benefits!

The same thing is true of tithing: Most people in

churches don't understand the benefits of tithing.

"That's *Old* Testament," they argue. "We're under the New Covenant. We don't believe in tithing."

"You're really in trouble," I tell them. "It's a shame you come and worship God, yet you live on Barely-Make-It Street until the day you die and go to Glory, where there are streets of gold."

You can have the benefits of prosperity if you tithe, and the Lord promised to rebuke the devourer from you. So pay your "premium" — your tithe. If you don't pay your "premium," you won't get any benefits. That's the way I look at tithing. (This part never goes over very big!)

My Vision of Jesus on the Cross

Getting back to the Communion service, as one of the deacons, I was standing up front holding the emblems and assisting.

I was really hungry for God, and I prayed, "God, I want revelation knowledge of what we're doing in this service."

You see, sometimes we do things "religiously," according to traditions we've become accustomed to. But people don't necessarily understand our traditions.

Pastors ought to spend an entire service teaching on why we receive Communion so people will understand what it's all about and what its benefits are.

Paul, one of the greatest apostles who ever lived, said he was determined to know nothing but Jesus Christ and Him crucified. I was determined to find out why we were receiving Communion!

As I was standing there, pondering this and praying, "God, I really want to know what took place at Calvary," it seemed like the roof came off that beautiful new sanctuary — and there was Calvary!

I saw Jesus hanging on the cross, with the crown of thorns on His head, the wound in His side, and the blood flowing out of His wounds. I said, "Yes, I recognize that."

But God said to me, "The pictures you see in Sunday School and in cathedrals aren't really what Jesus looked like on the cross."

Demonic Diseases Hit Jesus!

Suddenly reality started breaking through to me. I saw words fly through the air out of heaven and hit Jesus, and He flinched as they struck Him.

The word "cancer" would hit Him, and He would flinch.

"Arthritis" would hit Him, and He would flinch.

"Tuberculosis" would hit Him — and all of a sudden, the words came faster and faster. All kinds of diseases started hitting Him so fast, I couldn't even make out their names.

Every time one hit my Savior, He started changing. He didn't even look like a man; He just looked like a disease. It was horrible! When I saw that, I said, "He doesn't even look like a man."

These words kept hitting Him — every demonic disease on earth hit Him. That's how our sickness and disease were laid on Him.

All of a sudden, He no longer looked like the Catholic art work I grew up seeing. All of a sudden, He no longer even looked like a man! Why? Because the Word of God says that the curse of the law was laid on Him.

He took the sins of the world upon Himself for us. In a sense, He paid our "premiums" for us, and now we can enjoy all the benefits of Calvary!

I Saw What Really Happened at Calvary!

That vision really made a preacher out of me, because *I saw what really happened at Calvary!*

I saw that Jesus bore *all* my sicknesses and diseases, like the Word of God says.

That vision is as fresh to me today as when I had it more than 20 years ago. That's why I refuse to accept it if someone tries to tell me that the Lord puts sickness and disease on us to teach us something! That's a miscarriage of justice!

And I refuse to take anything from the devil when he tries to put pain, weakness, or disease on me. I tell him, "No! Those things were already laid on Jesus two thousand years ago!"

You see, those are some of the benefits of Calvary. As Paul said, I don't want to know anything but Jesus Christ and Him crucified.

What Paul meant was, we Christians need to go back to Calvary and discern what Jesus provided for us — the benefits of Calvary — and walk in those privileges. Let's not walk below our blood-bought privileges!

Let's not forget that *there's a Healer in the house!*

Prosperity: One of the Benefits of Calvary

I was preaching for a Hispanic pastor once, and he invited another Hispanic pastor to have lunch with us. "This other pastor would like to talk to you," he explained.

"That's fine," I said. "I'd love to talk to him. I like to minister to ministers."

I do a great deal of counseling with ministers because I have a traveling ministry, but I don't counsel with people from their churches or their staff members. I tell them to go to their pastor, because their shepherd is the one who should counsel them.

I never got to talk much to the pastor who wanted me to talk to him because *he* did all the talking. I ate my salad and then I ate my hamburger, and still he talked and talked.

Finally he said, "I want to ask you a question" — but he didn't actually ask me a question. Instead, he informed me, "I just don't understand it: I preach on Sundays, but I still have to work a secular job for a living."

"How many do you have in your church," I interjected.

"Oh, we've got about 300."

"And you still have to work?"

Then he launched into a big discussion, telling me, "We Hispanics are all poor. Our families came from Mexico, and we've known only poverty through all our generations." He went on and on in this vein.

Finally he stopped. As I wiped my face with my napkin, he said, "That's my problem."

The Pastor Who Preached Poverty

It was my turn. I said, "First of all, your church isn't your problem; *you're* the problem the church has! Your skin may be brown, but the blood of Jesus Christ erased racial distinctions."

Next I told this pastor, "I can just imagine what you tell your congregation when you receive the offering."

"What do I say?"

"You tell them, 'I know you work in the fields, and I know you don't have much money, but if you could give *something*, it would really help.'"

The pastor exploded, "How did you know? You must be a mind reader!"

I said, "No, I didn't even have to get that by the Spirit. All I had to do was listen to you talk. *You talk poverty.* Poverty has followed the Hispanic people here from Mexico. You need to teach your people that when they receive Jesus Christ as their personal Savior, they have come into a new family.

"They're now children of the King, *and they need to appropriate the benefits of Calvary.* One of those benefits is that they don't need to be poor anymore, and they don't need to allow that poverty spirit to get on them."

Controlling Wrong Thinking

He got mad at me. "Well, Brother Dufresne," he said, "when *you* got saved I guess all your wrong thinking left immediately, and your mind became clear."

"No," I told him. "I hear testimonies of that happening to people, but my mind tried to get even *more* squirrely! I became born again, but this body and this mind didn't."

People ask me, "What's your family background? What's your family tree?"

I say, *"Nuts.* Nuts on my mother's side and nuts on my father's side." But when I made Jesus Christ Lord of my life, that "nut tree" died instantly, and I became a child of the King!

The Bible tells us to do something with our *body:* Keep it under control. It also tells us to renew our *mind* with the Word of God.

It's our responsibility. I'm the one who had to get hold of that squirrely mind of mine and get it renewed in the Word and under control.

If a bad thought comes, I don't put up with it. I cast it

down. I say, "No, that isn't *my* thought, devil, in the Name of Jesus."

People tell me, "I don't know what to do with my thought life. I just can't control it."

Yes, you can. The Bible says for you to do something about your mind unless you've got a devil in there that you need to have cast out.

Men Who Saw Calvary

I've been enjoying the benefits of Calvary since the day I got saved. Eventually I got T.L. Osborn's book *Healing the Sick*. In the book, he explained that the curse of sickness has been laid on Jesus. I said, "That's what I saw! That's what I saw! That's what I saw!" I had a vision of Calvary and what was provided for me.

Another man who had the same vision long before Jesus went to the cross was Isaiah, an Old Testament prophet.

In Isaiah 53:1-11, Isaiah wrote prophetically that the Messiah was so marred, He didn't even look like a man. He wasn't beautiful, like we assume the Son of God to be.

The "man of sorrows" who hung on the cross became sin. He became sickness and disease. He became poverty. He carried all these things for you and me so we wouldn't have to carry them.

So why are you carrying a heavy load?

"Well, I'm doing it for the Lord," many answer piously.

No, Jesus already carried it. *Do you think you're better than Jesus? Are you trying to be your own Savior?"*

You're not in that category; however, you are a joint-heir with Jesus Christ if you're one of His.

Preachers Who Slap Jesus!

The way some preachers preach, do you know what they're doing? The Lord showed me this amazing scene one day.

It's as if they get a ladder, lean it against the cross, climb up there, wearing the traditions of men that state that Jesus didn't bear all our sickness and disease — and reach out and slap Jesus in the face as they call Him a liar!

That's what a lot of preachers are actually doing as they're preaching doubt and unbelief from their pulpits!

As for me, I don't want to know anything but Jesus Christ and Him crucified. That includes the benefits of our redemption — like having a Healer in the house!

Chapter 5

The Benefits of Communion

For I have received of the Lord that which also I delivered unto you, That the Lord Jesus the same night in which he was betrayed took bread:

And when he had given thanks, he brake it, and said, Take, eat: this is my body, which is broken for you: this do in remembrance of me.

1 Corinthians 11:23,24

Jesus said, "This is my body, which is broken for you: this do *in remembrance* of me." Notice He did not say, *"in memory* of me." There's a big difference. "In remembrance" means, when taking Communion, remember what was provided for you.

Most people take Communion *"in memory of* poor Jesus." They may even shed a few tears, feeling sorry for Him, hanging on that cross.

But Jesus isn't dead; He was resurrected! And He's no longer hanging on that cross; He's seated at the right hand of the Father, doing fine. He isn't even poor anymore; He's in heaven, a place of indescribable wealth, where no one wants for anything.

So Jesus isn't telling you to take Communion *in memory of Him*; He's telling you to do it *in remembrance of Him*.

Three Areas To Put in Remembrance

There are three areas you need to put in remembrance.

First, I like to *put God in remembrance*. He said so: "Put

47

me in remembrance of my Word." You put Him in remembrance by saying, "Father, your Word says, 'By his stripes I was healed two thousand years ago.'"

Sometimes I interview people who are in the healing line. I ask them, "What is going to happen when I lay hands on you?"

"Well, I hope I'm going to get my healing," they usually say.

"No, you already got it two thousand years ago!"

The devil either puts you in the future tense or in the past tense, but "now faith is." Faith is always *now*, in the present tense. It isn't in the future, and it isn't in the past. It's always *now!* We live in it *now!* It's ours *now!* Why? Because faith *is.* If it isn't *now*, it isn't faith.

If it's in the future, it's *hope.* If it's in the past, it's *history.* Too many people live in history. "Poor ol' Jesus," they sigh. "One of these days — in the sweet by-and-by — I'll be healed."

I want to live *now!* Healing has been provided for me *now.* It's fresh for me *now.* It's mine *now.* I'm walking in healing *now.* *There's a Healer in the house!*

"Well, you don't look healed," grumbles Unbelief. Look — you've still got those tumors."

"I'm healed because the Bible says I'm healed. My healing is not based on what my body says; it's based on what the Word of God says."

We're to put God in remembrance of what He provided for us.

Second, *I put the devil in remembrance* of what God said.

Third, *I put myself in remembrance* of the benefits of Calvary. When I receive Communion, it puts me in remembrance of the benefits of Calvary and of what Jesus provided for me there.

That's why Paul said, "I am determined not to know anything save Jesus Christ, and Him crucified."

Power Is in the Benefits of Calvary

The power of God is in the benefits of Calvary!

In our text, First Corinthians 2:1, we saw that Paul did not come to the Corinthians with eloquence of speech or wisdom. In verse 4, Paul says:

> **And my speech and my preaching was not with enticing words of man's wisdom, *but in demonstration of the Spirit and of power.***

Paul came with demonstration of that power because he said, "I am determined to know nothing but what was provided for me at Calvary."

You ought to study your Bible to find out everything that Jesus provided for you on Calvary. Then you can put yourself in remembrance of it.

Paul's teaching about Communion in First Corinthians 11 continues in verse 25:

> **After the same manner also he took the cup, when he had supped, saying, This cup is the new testament in my blood: this do ye, as oft as ye drink it, in remembrance of me.**

"Remembrance" means to remind, or to call to mind, the blood covenant that Jesus and the Father cut. And you have a right into that covenant, because Jesus Christ is your big Brother! Do you know that covenant can't be broken? The Father and the Son will not break that covenant.

This Is Christianity

That's why I believe the Hispanic pastor who was always talking about the poverty his people had known in the past should now begin teaching them the benefits of Calvary and who they are in Christ.

Yes, you may have come from a background of extreme poverty and extreme everything else — but the bondage of your background died when you accepted Christ. It died two thousand years ago!

Praise God, I was ready for a nut house, but I grabbed onto the benefits of Calvary. I learned that renewing my mind with the Word of God instills the mind of Christ in me, so I wouldn't have to be nuts.

This is the real thing! *This is Christianity.* This, right here, is what it's all about. This is "where the rubber meets the road."

I don't want to know anything but Jesus Christ. I am determined not to know anything except the benefits of Calvary.

How To Avoid the Ditch

The Lord said to me, "Weave the benefits of the cross through your teaching and your preaching. If you stay with the benefits of the cross, you'll see people delivered, and you won't get in a ditch."

Calvary is where it all happened. That's where our benefits are.

When you teach out of the Old Testament, *always go through Calvary* with the teaching. It will keep your doctrine sound.

That's the trouble with what prophets are teaching today. If people would *go through Calvary*, they would understand that they don't need to go to a prophet for guidance like people did under the Old Testament.

When you *go through Calvary,* you've got the Holy Spirit. After Calvary, Jesus sent us the Holy Spirit to dwell in us and with us. He was only able to come to us because of what happened at Calvary. You're led by Him, not by a prophet.

The Perils of Disobedience

Traveling ministries get off when the minister gets tired. "Well, I'll go pastor some church for a while," he or she decides.

If you ask them, "Did God call you to pastor," they'll snap at you, "I don't care if He did or not — *I'm tired!* I'm going to go pastor."

They're in trouble if they do.

Fortunately for us, under the New Covenant, we're under grace. But under the Old Covenant, if an unqualified or sinful priest entered the Holy of Holies, he was struck dead immediately! It takes a little longer to die now.

I'm determined to run the race. When I'm 85 years old, I plan on still being strong in my mind, my body, and my calling. I expect to be preaching as long as the Lord tarries.

When Man's Nature Changes

When I got saved, my nature changed. I'm in God's family now. All that Ed Dufresne used to be is gone. I'm in Christ now. When I look at people, I purpose to see them through God's eyes.

I don't look at brown; I don't look at black; I don't look at white skin anymore. Praise God, I see Calvary, and I see that God has called me to preach. I'm enjoying the benefits of the cross.

Not everyone does, of course. They'll tell you, "You know, cancer (or some other terrible disease) runs in my family."

Which family? The old family, or the new family? It doesn't run in your *new* family! I'm going to walk in the new family. I'm going to take the benefits of the cross!

If that Hispanic pastor would just get hold of the benefits of Calvary and start teaching his people about tithing instead of working in the fields, they'd end up *owning* the fields!

When he says, "I know that you work hard, and I surely wouldn't want to ask you to pay your tithes," *he's robbing those people!*

If they would pay their tithes, they would prosper. Some of you don't like that because you don't like to tithe. I don't care. You can't fire me, because you didn't hire me. I work for God.

"Let a Man Examine Himself"

Continuing our study of Communion:

> For as often as ye eat this bread, and drink this cup, ye do shew the Lord's death till he come.
>
> Wherefore whosoever shall eat this bread, and drink this cup of the Lord, unworthily [with the wrong spirit], shall be guilty of the body and blood of the Lord.
>
> But let a man examine himself, and so let him eat of that bread, and drink of that cup.
>
> For he that eateth and drinketh unworthily, eateth and drinketh damnation to himself, not discerning the Lord's body.

> For this cause many are weak and sickly among
> you, and many sleep [die].
>
> 1 Corinthians 11:26-30

We need to teach people to make sure they're right with God before they receive Communion. Why? Because the blood speaks out and reveals sin.

A worldly spirit has gotten into the Church. The way people live and behave has almost become a "game." For example, people who are secretly committing adultery come to church.

When I pastored, I would state during a Communion service, "If you're living in adultery, do not take Communion, because the blood speaks out. We're not to trample underfoot the blood of Jesus."

True Worship Will Come

Most pastors let everyone who's saved — and even those who aren't — take Communion. But God is raising up a Church in these last days that will know how to worship Him.

Remember the woman at the well? She told Jesus, "The Jews worship God one way, and we Samaritans worship God another way." Jesus replied, "But the hour cometh, and now is, when the true worshippers shall worship the Father in spirit and in truth: for the Father seeketh such to worship him" (John 4:23).

I believe these are the last days, when believers are going to enter into true worship, the glory cloud will come in, the power of God will fall, and everyone in the building will be healed. It's going to happen. I can see it! *There's a Healer in the house!*

Notice First Corinthians 11:28: "But let a man examine his neighbor, the preacher, and the preacher's kids." Is that what it says? No, it says, "But let a man examine *himself,* and so let him eat of that bread, and drink of that cup."

In Full Gospel-type churches, we've always examined ourselves to see if we have sin in our life, and that's good; that's one part of it. But here's another: As you study the cross references to these scriptures, you'll discover that Communion is a time for you to put yourself in remembrance, and then to examine yourself to see if you're in faith for the benefits of Calvary.

Remember: Communion is for your benefit. Jesus has already done everything He is going to do. Do you need healing in your body? Walk in the benefits of Calvary. Remember the blood covenant that has provided healing for you! *There's a Healer in the house!*

"Not Discerning the Lord's Body"

> For he that eateth and drinketh unworthily, eateth and drinketh damnation to himself, not discerning the Lord's body.
>
> For this cause many are weak and sickly among you, and many sleep [die].
>
> **1 Corinthians 11:29,30**

"...Eateth and drinketh damnation to himself, *not discerning the Lord's body."* The next verse begins, "For this cause...." What cause? Not discerning, or having insight into, the benefits that have been provided for you and me.

"For this cause, many are wimps — weak, and sickly among you — and many sleep." The true translation is, *"many die."*

Paul is addressing the Church. He isn't writing to sinners; he's talking to you and me, the Church, in this epistle.

If you go to the funeral of a Christian who was 35 years

old, they come under this passage of scripture. How would you like to preach this at a funeral: "'For this cause' is the reason they died, because they didn't appropriate the benefits of Calvary." But that's the truth.

We all have been promised long life. Not all of us are there — not everyone's faith is there. I understand that. It doesn't even mean they were bad people. It doesn't mean they went to hell. They went to heaven. They just didn't take the benefits that were provided for them.

Some people don't like to hear this preached, because they like to pet their sickness or disease. Some women like to be sick because it gets them attention from their husband — attention he won't give them unless they are sick. And vice versa.

"For This Cause Many Are Weak and Sickly"

"For this cause many are weak and sickly among you, and many sleep." They're weak in their body. They're sickly, and many die. That's just one part of it.

The other part, which I preach frequently to ministers and churches, concerns discerning and not discerning the gift ministries in the Body of Christ. (See First Corinthians chapters 11 through 14.) This is the spiritual part.

The physical part is the reason why many are sick: Because they do not discern the benefits Jesus provided for them on Calvary.

And because they do not discern that there's a Healer in the house!

Chapter 6

When We're Not Healed

"For this cause many are weak and sickly among you, and many sleep [die]." If we would judge ourselves, we would not be judged. But when we are judged, we are chastened of the Lord.

So we must judge ourselves: Are we in the faith? Are we taking the benefits that have been provided for us as children of God? I'm not addressing sinners; I'm addressing saints.

Now, don't get mad at me, but let's look at hospitals and doctors. No, I'm not against hospitals, and I'm not against doctors. I believe medicine and doctors have helped a lot of people. Praise God for them. Without them, a lot of us Christians would already be dead!

Now if you, as a Christian, are going to a doctor or are in need of a doctor, and that's where your faith is, continue to go. Never go beyond your faith. But desire to develop your faith for God's best, which is to live in divine health.

My point is, if we develop our faith, the hospitals and the doctors are not for us; they're God's grace for the sinner, because the believer has already been provided with God's provision.

Unfortunately, even though *there's a Healer in the house,* some are not able to receive this provision yet, because they don't believe it. "For this cause" — for not having insight into the benefits of what was provided for us at Calvary — they're not healed.

All the benefits of Calvary, including redemption, healing, prosperity, and long life, are present in the body and the blood of Communion! That's what Paul is talking about when he says we're not discerning what has been provided for us.

Take the Word's Prescription

"For this cause...." The reason people in the Body of Christ are sick is because they don't take the "prescription" of the Word of God. I know that's the reason. This knowledge is what set me free! Actually, this is what the Gospel is all about.

Let's tie this knowledge in with Isaiah 53, which is a prophetic look at Jesus, "the suffering Messiah," on the cross. "Who hath believed our report," Isaiah begins the first verse.

"Who hath believed our report?" Who can believe this? "And to whom is the arm of the Lord revealed? For he shall grow up before him as a tender plant, and as a root out of a dry ground..." (Isaiah 53:1,2).

Isaiah was describing Jesus when he prophesied, "...he hath no form nor comeliness; and when we shall see him, there is no beauty that we should desire him" (verse 2). In other words, Jesus didn't have a pleasing physical appearance.

Now look at Isaiah 52:14, where Isaiah paints a true portrait of Jesus on the cross: "As many were astonied [astonished] at thee; his visage [appearance] was so marred more than any man, and his form more than the sons of men."

When God Gave Healing on Credit

Do you remember in the first chapter of this book where we noted that the children of Israel were bitten by

58

snakes out in the wilderness — and they were healed "on credit" with their "Master Healing Card"? There was a Healer in their house!

This story is found in Numbers 21. Moses prayed, and God told him if a pole with a brass serpent was held up, all the sick who looked on it would be healed.

Why did they put *a snake* on that pole? Why didn't they put *a lamb*, which would have symbolized Jesus, the Lamb of God, their coming Messiah? The snake symbolized sin, and our sins were laid on Christ. He took our sins upon Himself.

They got healing "on credit" before Calvary!

Oh, healing *is* God's will for people! He even let the children of Israel get healing "on credit" — and then Jesus came and picked up the tab!

He hung on the cross to pay for it, and as He hung there, He *became* sin. He went to hell and paid the price for us.

The Essence of the Gospel

Religious people can't handle that. Their brain goes "tilt"! But that's the essence of the Gospel. These truths are what Paul was referring to when he said, "I don't want to know anything but Him crucified."

This is where the power of God is! This is where you'll find deliverance that outshines mere religion.

"Religion" paints Jesus on the cross, bleeding — but it doesn't go any further than that!

I want you to know that Jesus didn't *stay* on that cross. He went to hell as our Substitute, and He paid the price for us. Then He rose again from the dead.

Now that I've accepted Him, no one can put that old

sin-nature of unrighteousness on me. I'm a child of the King now — not by my doing, but by God's.

Isaiah the Reporter

I saw that same vision Isaiah saw. I'm not bragging; it's a fact. I'm reporting what I saw, just like the prophet Isaiah did. He was a reporter.

So when I relate these things, all I'm doing is reporting. Can you see how preaching the benefits of the cross can keep your doctrine straight?

The devil has already been whipped, so the real fight is in pulling down strongholds, as God told us in His Word. And the biggest stronghold of all is in your mind. Get that mind of yours renewed according to the Word of God!

The Sorrows of Calvary

Isaiah reported that there was no beauty we would behold at Calvary. I know, because I saw Calvary. There was no beauty in Jesus. He was so marred, He didn't even resemble a man.

There was no beauty in His crown of thorns — it was an ugly thing — but religion really likes those thorns and the aspect of suffering.

Down in Mexico and over in the Philippines, people cut and beat themselves to try to atone for their sins. But Jesus already bore the sins of mankind!

We don't need to try to atone for our sins and, anyway, we *couldn't*, because we aren't Jesus. So why should we punish ourselves?

People wouldn't need to try to be their own Savior if we'd teach them that all they have to do is take the benefits of Calvary!

My dad told me for years, "Son, when I get my life straightened out, I'll accept Christ."

I said, "Dad, you'll never get it straightened out." You can never get better without Jesus. All you can do is accept by faith the benefits Jesus provided for you on Calvary.

"With His Stripes We Are Healed"

He is despised and rejected of men; a man of sorrows, and acquainted with grief: and we hid as it were our faces from him; he was despised, and we esteemed him not.

Surely he hath borne our griefs, [this means sickness and disease] and carried our sorrows: yet we did esteem him stricken, smitten of God, and afflicted.

But he was wounded for our transgressions, [our sins] he was bruised for our iniquities: the chastisement of our peace was upon him; and with his stripes we are healed.

Isaiah 53:3-5

Isaiah reported that Jesus was "despised and rejected of men; a man of sorrows, and acquainted with grief" (verse 3). If you're preaching what I'm preaching, you're going to be despised and rejected, too, because you'll be preaching the same message Paul preached.

Do you know who is going to despise and reject you? Christians — religious people. But God never called us to try to straighten each other out or fight one another using our sermons as weapons.

I want that faith and anointing Paul had, where snakes bit him and he just shook them off, unharmed.

Now notice the seventh verse: "He was oppressed, and he was afflicted, yet he opened not his mouth: he is brought as a lamb to the slaughter, and as a sheep before her shearers is dumb, so he openeth not his mouth."

Beating the Blues

I've made up my mind that if I begin to be oppressed, I'll say, "No! I'm going to have a good day. I'm not going to have a blue Monday." At such times, I speak to my mind, "You're not going to be blue."

"Yeah, but you have a right to be blue," it tells me.

"No, I don't have a right to be blue."

"But everything is going wrong."

"I'm not going to receive it."

I'm determined not to accept any other knowledge. I choose to receive only positive knowledge. That's another benefit of Calvary.

The only way to really help people today is to stay out of theological ditches and go through Calvary in your preaching. Look at things in the light of Calvary, through the New Covenant.

Jesus *is* coming again — I don't care what others preach. I've made up my mind I'm going to preach Jesus and Him crucified, plus the benefits of Calvary. I want that anointing on my life that I need to help people.

I want to tell them, *"There's a Healer in the house!"*

Chapter 7

God Is Glorified in Healing

Sin and sickness are from the same source. That's why Jesus said to the man in Matthew 8, "Thy *sins* be forgiven thee."

God is glorified in healing, not in sickness.

Some people say that God allows people to be sick so believers can lay hands on them and they will recover. They say that if there were no sick people, we wouldn't know that God heals. But we are to believe what the Bible tells us, not what we see around us.

We know that God heals, because His Word says so! We don't have to see it to believe it. We *know* there's a Healer in the house!

God doesn't have to plan sickness for anyone so He can get glory when they are healed. There are already enough people who are under Satan's authority for us to pray for and lay hands on for healing.

Christians should all be well and sharing with sinners how they can be born again and healed. Christians should also be learning more and more each day from God's Word. When we do, we will discover this truth:

God wants everyone to be well!

Methods of Healing

God desires so much for you to be healed that He has established several methods by which you can be healed.

Therefore, by acting on His Word, it is possible for every person to be healed!

But first you must know it *is* God's will to heal you. Listed below are some scriptures that clearly establish the fact that it is the will of God to heal. Get your Bible and read the scriptures listed below. Remember, God is no respecter of persons!

John 14:7,8 — Jesus' ministry was an expression of God's will. He never turned anyone down who came to Him for healing.

Luke 5:12,13 — Jesus said that it was His will to heal this man.

Luke 11:17 — God's kingdom is not a divided house. God doesn't want some people sick and others well. God and the devil are not working together to teach His children something through sickness. The Holy Spirit is the Teacher. God wants you well; it's Satan who wants you sick.

Acts 10:38 — Sickness is oppression from the devil.

Isaiah 53:4-10 — Jesus bore your sicknesses and your chastisement (punishment by pain) so you wouldn't have to experience them.

Listed below are methods of healing with the scriptural basis for each method.

1. Anoint With Oil (James 5:14-16)

In his epistle, James is addressing newly born-again people. The anointing with oil was established to give those who have little or no knowledge of God's Word about healing something tangible.

They can feel the oil and hear the elders' prayer of faith, and thus are better able to receive their healing. This method is also good for Christians who are more mature but whose Word level is low.

2. The Prayer of Agreement (Matthew 18:19,20)

The prayer of agreement is having another person believe with you and agree for your healing. This method is only effective if you make sure the other person will believe and stand firm with you on God's Word.

When you and the other person are in genuine agreement, you will encourage one another with God's Word.

3. The Laying on of Hands (Mark 16:17,18; Mark 5:21-23)

If someone lays hands on you for healing, he should be someone who believes that when he lays his hands on you, you will recover.

You should also release your faith as Jairus did in Mark 5:21-23. He believed that when Jesus laid His hands on his sick daughter, she would recover.

You don't need to go to a service where a minister has a healing ministry to be healed by the laying on of hands, although that is a good way to be healed.

Actually, any Christian who believes that when he lays hands on the sick, they will recover can be used by God in this way.

4. The Gifts of Healing (1 Corinthians 12:8-11; Acts 3:1-8; John 5:1-9; John 9:1-7; 2 Kings 5:9-14)

The gifts of healing mentioned in First Corinthians 12:9 operate as the Holy Spirit wills. As you can see from reading the above scripture references, the Holy Spirit uses a person who will be obedient to get healing to the person in need.

The Holy Spirit knows what it takes to get that person to release his faith and receive healing (as in the case of Elisha and Naaman).

There are different operations, as the Bible says, but it is all as the Holy Spirit wills. Sometimes He will heal as someone ministers in music, as the psalmist David did. Often He has ministers call out that people are being healed, getting healing to them in that manner. There are many operations of the gifts of healing, and all are wonderful.

5. *Special Anointings (Acts 19:11,12; Acts 10:38; Mark 5:25-34; Matthew 14:34-36; Mark 3:10,11)*

Kenneth E. Hagin says, "The laying on of hands can also be practiced from the standpoint of transmission. By laying on of hands, one transmits God's healing power unto those sick persons, because he is anointed with that power."

Notice that this power does not work *automatically.* You cannot transfer healing power to whomever you will. Jesus Himself could not heal people who had no faith! (See Mark 6:5.)

The Touch of Faith

When the woman with the issue of blood touched Jesus and He felt healing power go out of Him, He asked, "Who touched my clothes?" His disciples replied, "Thou seest the multitude thronging thee, and sayest thou, Who touched me?" (Mark 5:30,31).

There was no way of telling how many people had touched Him out of curiosity, just to see if anything would happen. But no *healing power* had flowed out of Him into any of them; only into the woman who touched Him with faith, recognizing there was a Healer in that place.

> And he looked round about to see her that had done this thing.
>
> But the woman fearing and trembling, knowing what was done in her, came and fell down

before him, and told him all the truth.

And he said unto her, Daughter, thy faith hath made thee whole....

Mark 5:32-34

6. Just Say It (Mark 11:23; Matthew 8:5-13; Mark 5:25-28)

The last two methods of receiving healing are the operation of the God-kind of faith. God spoke the world into being by faith (Hebrews 11:3).

Jesus said in Mark 11:23 that "whosoever" can do the same thing. This means, you can speak your healing into being, believe it in your heart, and it will come to pass!

7. Believing You Receive When You Pray (Mark 11:24; Hebrews 11:1; 1 Peter 2:24)

Jesus said to believe you receive the things you desire *when you pray.* Faith says, "I am healed now, according to God's Word." Receiving your healing by faith, based on God's Word, will bring the manifestation of that healing to your body.

Ephesians 6:13,14 teaches us to keep standing on God's Word. Once you believe you have received your healing by faith, you are to stand, regardless of what you feel like. Jesus promised that if you believe you receive it when you pray, it will come to pass.

Praying for Life-and-Death Situations

In Isaiah 54:17, Gods Word says that no weapon that is formed against us shall prosper, and that every tongue that shall rise against us in judgment we shall show to be in the wrong.

Here is a confession of faith that will prove invaluable when you are faced with believing that someone will live and receive their healing when everyone around you is saying it is impossible for them to live.

For example, there are times when doctors say there is nothing that can be done for a patient, and this person is sure to die.

However, you can stand on God's Word and proclaim that this weapon — death — that has been formed against them will not prosper, and that though tongues have risen against them, judging that they will die, they will show those judgments to be wrong — and they will live!

When you are praying for life-and-death situations, do what Jesus did in Mark 11:14. He spoke directly to the fig tree. And He spoke the end result. So speak directly to the body of the person that you are praying for, and tell that body to live! Tell it that there's a Healer in that house.

Remember: There is no distance in the spirit realm. You don't have to be with the person to speak life to them. Do what Jesus said to do in Mark 11:23: Speak to death and command it to leave, in the Name of Jesus!

Then, like He said to do in verse 24, believe that you receive life for that person when you pray. Then believe it's done because of faith in God's Word. God is not a man that He should lie.

From that time on, return God's Word to Him in prayer. His Word does not return to Him without producing an effect; it accomplishes what He purposes, and it prospers in the thing for which He sent it.

When praying for others, confess His Word over the situation like this:

A Healing Confession for Others

"Father, in the Name of Jesus, I thank you that _____ shall not die, but shall live and declare your works and recount your illustrious acts. And, although this is impossible with men, it is not impossible with You, for all things are possible with You.

68

"I will not weaken in faith and consider _____ 's body. No unbelief or distrust will make me waver or question concerning your promise, but I am strong and empowered by faith as I give praise and glory to You, for I am fully satisfied and assured that You are able and mighty to keep your Word and to do what You have promised.

"Your Word says that You will even deliver the one for whom I intercede who is not innocent through the cleanness of my hands. Whether the people I pray for are innocent or not, I believe that it is done because of my intercession, because You are no respecter of persons. I thank You that it is done in Jesus' Name. Amen. So be it!"

As you use this prayer from the Word of God, you will see results. Jeremiah 1:12 says that God is alert and active, watching over His Word to perform it. Expect Him to work in your behalf because He loves you.

Scripture References: Psalm 119:18; Mark 10:27; Romans 4:19-21; Job 22:30 (The Amplified Bible).

A Personal Healing Confession

"Father, in the Name of Jesus, I praise You that Jesus Himself took my weaknesses and infirmities and bore away my diseases. Because of this, and in agreement with Mark 11:24, I pray and believe that I am healed now!

"According to your Word, Jesus personally bore my sins in His own body to the tree as to an altar and offered Himself on it, that I might cease to exist in sin and live in righteousness, and by His wounds I have been healed!

"My faith in your Word is my proof that I am healed, regardless of what my body says. I speak right now to my body and command that you get in line with the Word of God that says you have been healed. Now you act healed, look healed, sound healed, feel healed, taste healed, and smell healed, in the Name of Jesus!

"I thank You, Father, that it is done now! I will not weaken in faith and consider my body. No unbelief or distrust will make me waver or doubtingly question concerning your Word; but I am strong and empowered by faith, and I give praise and glory to You in Jesus' Name, because I am fully satisfied that You are able and mighty to keep your Word and do what You have promised."

Scripture References: Matthew 8:17; Mark 11:23,24; Romans 4:19-21.

Remember: *There's a Healer in the house!*